Learning to Read, Step by Step!

Ready to Read   Preschool–Kindergarten
• big type and easy words • rhyme and rhythm • picture clues
For children who know the alphabet and are eager to
begin reading.

Reading with Help   Preschool–Grade 1
• basic vocabulary • short sentences • simple stories
For children who recognize familiar words and sound out
new words with help.

Reading on Your Own   Grades 1–3
• engaging characters • easy-to-follow plots • popular topics
For children who are ready to read on their own.

Reading Paragraphs   Grades 2–3
• challenging vocabulary • short paragraphs • exciting stories
For newly independent readers who read simple sentences
with confidence.

Ready for Chapters   Grades 2–4
• chapters • longer paragraphs • full-color art
For children who want to take the plunge into chapter books
but still like colorful pictures.

STEP INTO READING® is designed to give every child a successful
reading experience. The grade levels are only guides; children will progress
through the steps at their own speed, developing confidence in their reading.
The F&P Text Level on the back cover serves as another tool to help you
choose the right book for your child.

Remember, a lifetime love of reading starts with a single step!

The quotations in this book come from Hillary Clinton's speeches and interviews and her two memoirs, *Living History* and *Hard Choices.*

For Jack, Nate, Adelaide, and Azzaria—no ceilings!
—S.C.

Grateful acknowledgment is made to Katie Dersnah Mitchell and Tish (McCoy) Dersnah for their help in researching Hillary Clinton's high school years.
Special thanks also go to Herbert Ragan, archivist at the William J. Clinton Presidential Library.

Text copyright © 2016 by Shana Corey
Illustrations copyright © 2016 by Adam Gustavson

All rights reserved. Published in the United States by Random House Children's Books, a division of Penguin Random House LLC, New York.

Step into Reading, Random House, and the Random House colophon are registered trademarks of Penguin Random House LLC.

Photograph credits: Cover: Getty Images/Ethan Miller; p. 3: Flickr/some rights reserved by Keith Kissel; pp. 6 (top), 20, 23, 24, 25, 30, 31, 32–33, 37: courtesy of the William J. Clinton Presidential Library; p. 6 (middle): courtesy of the U.S. Department of State; p. 6 (bottom): Wikimedia Commons; p. 21: courtesy of the Butler Center for Arkansas Studies, Central Arkansas Library System; p. 27: Getty Images/David Hume Kennerly; pp. 40–41: Flickr/some rights reserved by Marc Nozell; p. 42 (top): courtesy of the U.S. Department of State; p. 42 (bottom): Wikimedia Commons; p. 43: courtesy of the U.S. Department of State/Eric Bridiers; p. 45: AP/Susan Walsh; p. 47: Getty Images/Spencer Platt; p. 48: Getty Images/*The Washington Post.*

We have made every effort to trace the ownership of all copyrighted material and to secure permission from copyright holders. In the event of future questions arising as to the use of any material, we will be pleased to make all necessary corrections in subsequent printings.

Visit us on the Web!
StepIntoReading.com
randomhousekids.com

Educators and librarians, for a variety of teaching tools, visit us at RHTeachersLibrarians.com

Library of Congress Cataloging-in-Publication Data is available upon request.
ISBN 978-1-101-93235-3 (trade) — ISBN 978-1-101-93236-0 (lib. bdg.) —
ISBN 978-1-101-93237-7 (ebook)

Printed in the United States of America

10 9 8 7 6 5 4 3 2 1

This book has been officially leveled by using the F&P Text Level Gradient™ Leveling System.

HILLARY CLINTON

The Life of a Leader

by Shana Corey

illustrations by Adam Gustavson

Random House 🏠 New York

It is the early 1960s.
The United States
is working to send
astronauts to the moon.
A young girl
looks up at the stars.

She writes a letter to NASA

and volunteers

to be an astronaut.

NASA writes back.

The agency says it does not accept girls

into the space program.

But no one can stop

this girl from dreaming.

The world is changing.

And she will help change it.

She will grow up to be

the First Lady

of the United States,

a U.S. senator,

and the secretary

of state.

But she started out

as a regular kid—

just like you.

This is her story.

Hillary Rodham was born
in Chicago, Illinois,
on October 26, 1947.
She lived with her mother,
her father,
and her two younger brothers.
She played
kickball and softball.

She ice-skated
and rode her bike.

She was a Girl Scout
and went to church.
And she was a fan of
the New York Yankees!

Hillary's parents taught her
to work hard
and never quit.
Her father
loved politics,
and soon Hillary did too.

They discussed and debated
around the kitchen table.
Hillary learned
that it's okay to disagree.
But if you believe
in something,
you should be able
to defend it.

Hillary's mother had
a hard childhood.
She taught her children
that every human being matters
and everyone deserves a chance.
She taught Hillary to work
to make the world better.
She taught her
the importance of kindness.
Young Hillary took action.
She organized fund-raisers.
She babysat for the children
of poor farmworkers
so their parents could work.

Hillary loved school.

And she was always a leader.

In elementary school,

she was co-captain

of the safety patrol.

In high school,

Hillary began speaking out.

She joined the student council.

She planned pep rallies

and homecoming parades and proms.

She even took part

in a mock presidential debate!

Hillary attended Wellesley College.

She studied political science.

When Martin Luther King Jr.

was assassinated,

Hillary joined a protest march.

She spent a summer working

in the U.S. Congress.

America was at war in Vietnam,

and Hillary worried about

the country's future.

But she believed that

the government

could change things

for the better.

And she wanted to help.

The other students chose Hillary
to be the first student ever
to speak at the college's graduation.

After she graduated,
Hillary went to
Yale Law School.
She wanted
to use the law
to help children.

She volunteered to give
free legal advice
to the poor.
She represented children
in foster care.

Hillary fell in love
with a fellow law student
named Bill Clinton.
After graduation,
Hillary and Bill
moved to Arkansas
and got married.

Like Hillary,

Bill believed that government

could help people.

So he ran for

governor of Arkansas—

and won!

Hillary was very busy.
As the First Lady
of Arkansas,
she worked to make education
better in her state.
She also became
the first woman partner
at her law firm.

And she and Bill

had a little girl.

They named her Chelsea.

In 1992,

Bill ran for president

of the United States.

Hillary crisscrossed the country

campaigning for him.

Bill won the election!
Hillary became
the First Lady
of the United States.

Hillary was a new kind
of First Lady.
She set up an office
in the West Wing
of the White House,
where the president
had his office.

No First Lady

had done that before.

She tried to make it

easier for Americans

to get health care.

Hillary did not succeed

at everything.

And not everyone liked her.

When Hillary felt discouraged,
she thought about
her heroes.
"If you are scared,
keep going,"
Harriet Tubman
once said.
"Grow skin like a rhinoceros,"
Eleanor Roosevelt said.
Hillary remembered her parents'
lessons to be tough
and not to quit.

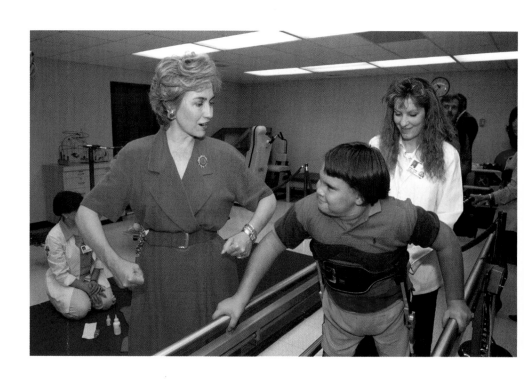

No matter

how hard life got,

she kept working.

As First Lady,

Hillary worked

to make it easier

for children

to go to preschool

and to get health care.

She wrote a newspaper column
and a book.
And she traveled.
Sometimes she
took Chelsea with her.

She also spoke out

for women's rights.

In 1995,

she gave a speech in Beijing, China.

"Women's rights

are human rights," she said.

The crowd gave her

a standing ovation.

After eight years
as First Lady,
Hillary had to decide
what to do next.
One day,
she spoke at a school
in New York City.
The theme of the event
was "Dare to Compete."
The captain of the girls'
basketball team introduced her.
"Dare to compete,"
she whispered to Hillary.

For years,

Hillary had encouraged women

to make their voices heard.

And so she decided

to run for the Senate.

A Senate seat was open

in New York state,

so she moved there.

She traveled all over the state—

from big cities to tiny towns.

She listened to voters

and wanted to make

their lives better.

On November 7, 2000,
Hillary became the first
First Lady to be elected
to public office.
She was also New York's
first woman senator.

In 2007,
Hillary decided to run
for president.
She didn't get
the nomination that year.
But many people were excited
about the possibility
of the United States'
first woman president.

"If we can blast
fifty women into space,
we will someday
launch a woman
into the White House,"
Hillary said.

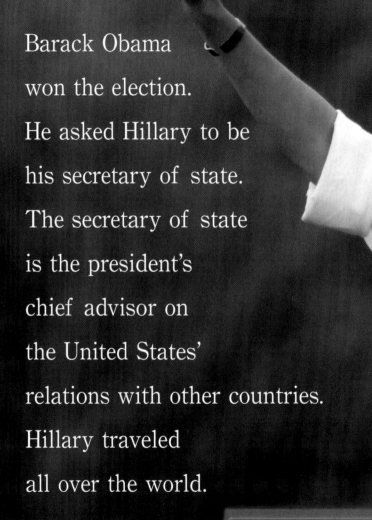

Barack Obama
won the election.
He asked Hillary to be
his secretary of state.
The secretary of state
is the president's
chief advisor on
the United States'
relations with other countries.
Hillary traveled
all over the world.

UNITE FO
CHANG

She met with

sultans and schoolchildren,

politicians and presidents.

And she continued to speak out

for women and children,

and for human rights for everyone.

"Leadership . . .

means standing up

for the dignity

of all your citizens,"

she said.

In 2013,

Hillary's term

as secretary of state ended.

She had visited

112 countries,

more than any

secretary of state before her.

She had brought increased

attention to women's rights

and other human rights.

And she had

traveled as many miles

as it would take

to get to the moon and back—

twice!

Hillary's work wasn't over, though.
On April 12, 2015,
Hillary announced
she would run for president again.
Over the next months,
people all across the country
listened to her speak
and joined her campaign.
"I've spent my life
fighting for children,
families,
and our country," she said.
"And I'm not stopping now."

She described the America
she believes in—
an America that includes
everyone.

Will Hillary be
the first woman to become
president of the United States?
Whatever happens,
Hillary has always believed
there are no limits
to what people can do.
And that includes YOU!